AWAKEN TRUST
TRANSFORM LIVE

Poems and Affirmations for
Inner-Growth and Self-Awareness

BY SMRITI AGRAWAL PHD

WWW.SMRITIAGRAWAL.COM

Dear Lynsey,
So lovely to meet
you. keep on smiling

Best,
Smriti

 FriesenPress

One Printers Way
Altona, MB R0G 0B0
Canada

www.friesenpress.com

Copyright © 2024 by Smriti Mona Agrawal, PhD
First Edition — 2024

www.smritiagrawal.com

ISBN
978-1-03-917659-1 (Hardcover)
978-1-03-917658-4 (Paperback)
978-1-03-917660-7 (eBook)

1. POETRY, SUBJECTS & THEMES, INSPIRATIONAL & RELIGIOUS

Distributed to the trade by The Ingram Book Company

Dedicated to my parents
and Sasha, my *shining star*.

PREFACE

This book is a collection of poem and affirmations that spontaneously appeared to me during my daily meditations; each loosely fit into one of these four human processes: *Awaken, Trust, Transform, Live.*

For me, these four processes have become pillars that broadly represent my path to growth as I dive deeper into my self-awareness and inward facing path. To truly experience it all "here and now" in the present moment, I needed to first *awaken* to everything. Awaken to who I am, all that I am. As this journey of awakening progressed, I began to embrace all parts of myself, be they painful or joyous, with compassion and gentleness.

As I began to awaken to it all, *Life* itself became personified. *She* became an imaginary inner best friend who brought me situations, experiences, and the confidence to know that all that is mine will not miss me. I started to *trust her.* This trust in *her* allowed me to witness and experience the abundance of all that is mine in every moment, and to let be all that no longer served my higher good or the highest good, making space for the new experiences to manifest.

With this complete trust in *Life*, the process of *transformation* began to unravel. Like a tightly wound ball of wool that had started to loosen and unwrap, I too began to loosen, slow down, scatter, and observe it all. My attention shifted to rest in higher mind from where I could allow compassion, kindness, peace, and love to permeate every pore of my being. Here I could hold space for myself and others and attend to human events with the beauty of spiritual response.

This is when I began to live, really live. I was no longer just surviving or getting by. I had moved from the space of contraction and tightness to that of expansion and looseness. I had shifted from continuous suffering to present joy. Feeling grateful for and forgiving everything and everyone here and now.

As you read this book, I urge you to allow it to move you into your inner spiritual realm, so you may uncover the inner beauty that already exists within and has been seeking you always. Let these lines introduce you to friendly and helpful parts of yourself so you may awaken too and trust your own spiritual story and journey.

CONTENTS

AWAKEN

Awaken to everything and all, as is here and now.

2

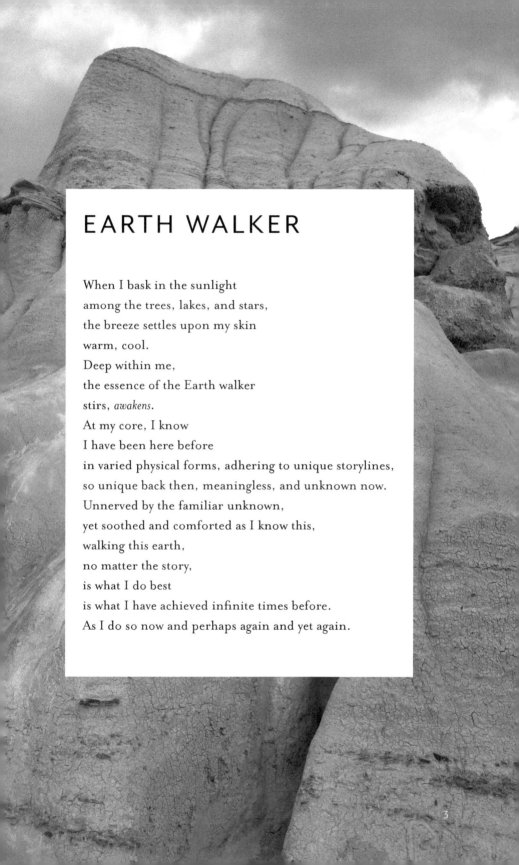

EARTH WALKER

When I bask in the sunlight
among the trees, lakes, and stars,
the breeze settles upon my skin
warm, cool.
Deep within me,
the essence of the Earth walker
stirs, *awakens*.
At my core, I know
I have been here before
in varied physical forms, adhering to unique storylines,
so unique back then, meaningless, and unknown now.
Unnerved by the familiar unknown,
yet soothed and comforted as I know this,
walking this earth,
no matter the story,
is what I do best
is what I have achieved infinite times before.
As I do so now and perhaps again and yet again.

4

EGO VS. LOVE

Ego sets up her elaborate shield to protect and distance. Love gently reaches in, to receive and connect.

ECLIPSED SUN

Each of us is an eclipsed sun,
our brightness covered
by eons of cultural conditioning.
Other people's opinions and lies,
have been used to draw inaccurate conclusions about ourselves.
Lies, which our mind finds many facts to validate.

As we begin to void the ego programs,
to see beyond the eclipse.
We see the sun in our true selves.
Our beauty, powerful and humble,
under the eclipse, simply shines
needing no validation for its true intensity.

PLAY

Play, is all we are here for,
Life brings us many props,
situations, objects, people to engage with,
each that comes and goes,
changes at varied paces.

If instead of becoming attached to,
identified with, afraid of these props
we choose to collaborate with loving curiosity, kind acceptance,
courage, and humor
letting go of what was and embracing what is.

Then such wonder the *play* would bring us.

INNER LABYRINTH

Overwhelmed and tempted
by external blame and shame,
I turn inward
to find my unending
ever mysterious inner labyrinth.
Its vast space, where I scatter and collect
as I map and charter its nonexistent edge—
herein lies my true peace.

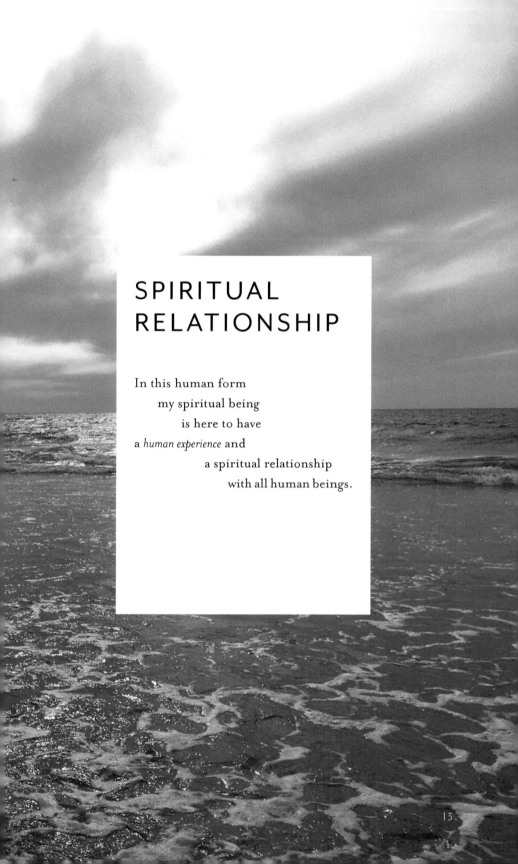

SPIRITUAL RELATIONSHIP

In this human form
    my spiritual being
       is here to have
a *human experience* and
        a spiritual relationship
         with all human beings.

THE REAL "ME"

I am the light at the center,
the Spirit and Conscious awareness.

In this human incarnate journey,
I adorn many labels and identities.

These varied stories and beliefs attach
human worth and value to me.
Allow me to be identified, categorized
understood.

While I graciously turn toward
and thank all my human karmic labels,
I constantly keep sight of the
light at the center, the real *me*.

FIELD OF BROKEN GLASS

With ego in possession of my inner self
the suffering equals to, her (ego)
stepping on my neck as she drags me
through a field of broken glass.

Incredible pain and unnecessary suffering.

If I allow this pain to awaken my inner self
I can gently bring awareness to all here and now
which brings me soft comfort and easy joy.
I can see small things available to me
which nourish my very soul.

And when ego anxiety is large,
I allow gratitude to permeate my whole being,
loving, healing all of me, here and now.

18

THE OBSERVER EFFECT

At center, my human remains
caught in karmic conditioning of
hate shame blame, tethered
by the thin veil of my ever
observing consciousness.

As my Spirit covers human and karma
in loving kindness and
unconditional friendliness,
the observer observers all.

The observer effects
subtly, altering every outcome.

TIME AND MONEY

Time and money are
 created by human ego,
  to serve only human ego.

   Awakening to human dependence
    on time and money,
     frees us from
      our servitude to human ego.

21

RISE UP

As a buoyant spiritual being
I am here to rise up.
I am here to transcend my human karma story.
I am here to collaborate with anyone dedicated
to do the same.
Sadly, leaving behind loved ones,
far too enmeshed in their human karma story.
For they are unprepared yet.

TRUST

Trust **her**, *trust* Life, *she is your one true best friend.*

TIME

Time, a human creation, organically doesn't exist,

So, what we believe to be the past, future, and parallel life stories
all co-exist now and here, in the present moment.

Sadly, our consciousness is tightly attached to this human form,
Bound by a veil, unable to break free or see beyond.

When we sleep, and as we dream, the veil of time lifts and thins,
allowing consciousness to transcend, be free and see it all occur
as it is, all at once.

THE INSTRUCTIONS

My human wanders the planet
in sorrow and ignorance,
asking desperately why she wasn't given
any instructions to living life.

The contents of enlightenment
gently remind her how,
her ever incarnating self, has been given
clear and compassionate
instructions to living a joyous life.

However, as this human continues to subscribe
to her ego musings,
the ability to discover and
comprehend the instructions to life,
became fully lost to her.

As a result, she wanders in
sorrow and ignorance.

Only once in a micro-moment when she looks beyond ego
with trust and delight,
does she discover with clarity,
the spirit language of living life.

THE ONE PERSON

I am here to help
that one person,

I am here to meet and fall in love
with that one person,

To care for, to carry,
the one person,

The one person who is *me*.

As I patiently love me,
compassionately accept me,
forgive my humanness
repeatedly,

I become more familiar,
to offering these very emotions
to any being outside of me.

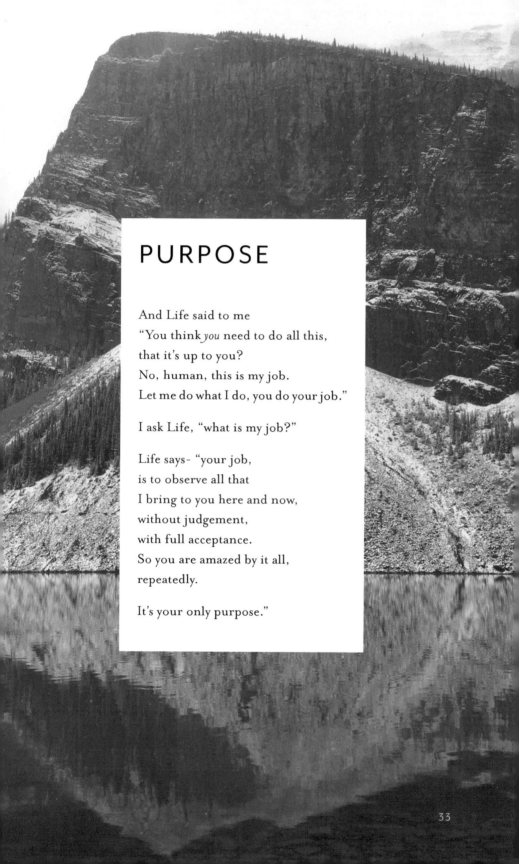

PURPOSE

And Life said to me
"You think *you* need to do all this,
that it's up to you?
No, human, this is my job.
Let me do what I do, you do your job."

I ask Life, "what is my job?"

Life says– "your job,
is to observe all that
I bring to you here and now,
without judgement,
with full acceptance.
So you are amazed by it all,
repeatedly.

It's your only purpose."

RIGHT

I am always the right person.
In the right place.
At the right time.
With the right things.
In the right life.
Right here and right now.

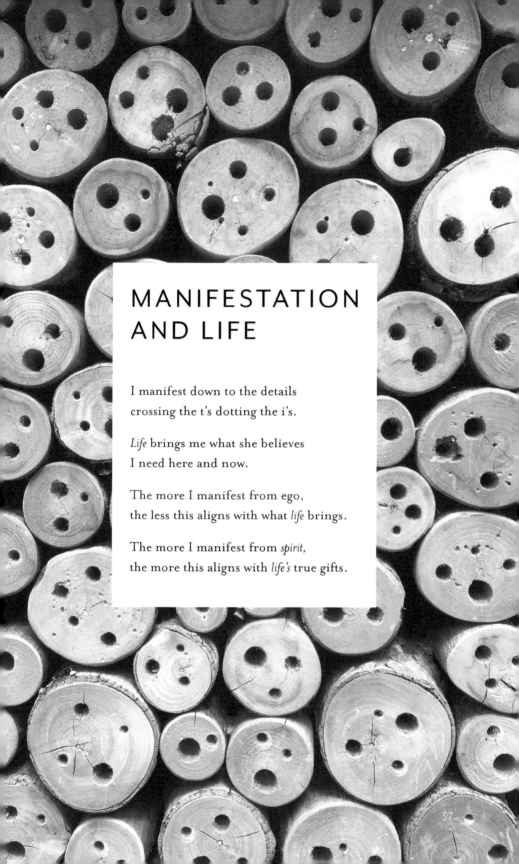

MANIFESTATION AND LIFE

I manifest down to the details
crossing the t's dotting the i's.

Life brings me what she believes
I need here and now.

The more I manifest from ego,
the less this aligns with what *life* brings.

The more I manifest from *spirit*,
the more this aligns with *life's* true gifts.

FLOW

As the earth holds me in her cradle
she gently whispers,

You belong,

You are enough,

You are worthy and valuable,

You are infinitely loved,

Your voice is important,

You are a highly evolving intuitive being,

You are powerful, a spiritually energetic human.

Then, she releases me into the eager welcoming arms of the vast universe.

ALL MY LOVE, TIME AND ENERGY

It is not the *object* of my desire
   which benefits from
      my love, time, and energy.

It is rather,
   the *part of me* that dares to desire,
      which greatly deserves all my love, time, and energy.

A LOVE LETTER
TO MY INNER CHILD

My love. You are most special to me,

I value and appreciate you.

You bring me absolute pleasure in simply being you.

Let me carry you, I can be your legs.
Rely on me, I will keep you safe.
Trust me, count on me, lean on me.
Allow yourself to be cared by me.
I will assist you; expect my help at all times.
It's ok to need me.

I am here now and always. I carry you, as *I love you.*

A NEED

See a need
fill a need.

When I try to fill a need
before I see the need,
no matter the extent of the effort exerted
the need remains unfulfilled.

When I see a need,
and I validate whether it is to be fulfilled.
I examine how it can be fulfilled.
I remain calmly in the space of the need.
It is only then, that I can truly fill the need.

A MUTE VESSEL

A musical instrument by itself is mute.
However, when played by a trusted musician,
they create a beautiful melody together.

The human vessel by itself is similarly mute.
It is quiet, until joined by its trusted spiritual self.
Once their trust grows to form an interdependent bond,
Then together, they create a magical tune.
A tune that flows into a collective orchestra,
an orchestra of the collective consciousness of this entire universe.

TRANSFORM

Transform into your spiritual self, the self having this human experience.

THE LOVING ENERGY EXCHANGE

When it's not serving the energy flow of the life you are building, release it, drop it, let it be.

Disappoint anyone and everyone easily disappointed, even if they will turn to others and turn away from you.

In a loving energy exchange, you will lean on others, as they lean on you, with an abundance of encouragement, honesty, acceptance, vulnerability, and open communication.

OBSERVE

I don't want to understand
or misunderstand.
I only want
to observe.

AIR IS LOVE

If air is pure *love*,

can it be
that today,

each of us,
breathes in *love*
for ourselves.

Breathe out *love*
to send to others.

COMFORT IN THE FAMILIAR

In a state of loneliness,
I seek comfort in familiarity.
I seek comfort in lower vibrational beings, even if
the encounter has always brought me hurt and suffering.

When I awaken to my state of loneliness,
I can bring myself to recognize, a healthier
happier, higher vibrational joy
ever present within me.

I can choose this higher, present moment joy,
than go to the default hurt and suffering.

This *transformation*, this
ascension, is the catalyst that
breaks the pattern of generational
suffering.
It creates in me a new joyous pattern.
A new habit which remains in me,
and is passed on to my next generation.

STILL

I remain still. Life comes and goes.

WORTH
AND VALUE

With desperation, I seek
my self-worth and value.

I search the external.
I grasp at old friendships.
At memories of beautiful times.
Pining, yearning, these
would return.
So, I may be valuable, whole again.

Exhausted in that search.
I drop it all.
Instead, I turn toward all that is
here now.
Everything that loves me and
allows itself to be loved by me.
I join my hands in humility.
I am eternally grateful for it all.

And just like that,
my worth and value shine through.
Right here, just the way it all is.
I am not clinging anymore, not
holding on.
Worth and value are here for me,
to know and behold.

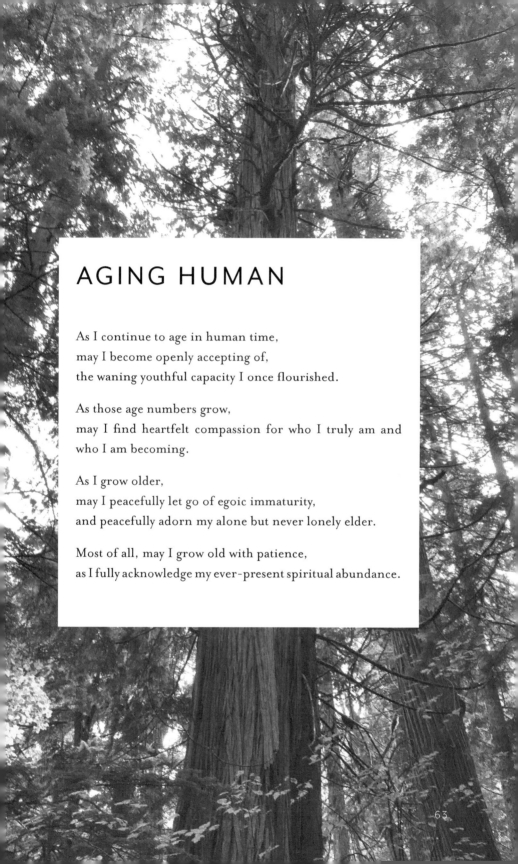

AGING HUMAN

As I continue to age in human time,
may I become openly accepting of,
the waning youthful capacity I once flourished.

As those age numbers grow,
may I find heartfelt compassion for who I truly am and
who I am becoming.

As I grow older,
may I peacefully let go of egoic immaturity,
and peacefully adorn my alone but never lonely elder.

Most of all, may I grow old with patience,
as I fully acknowledge my ever-present spiritual abundance.

WITH EVERY
CHOICE, I WIN

Equipped with no rulebook or set storyline to guide my life,
Each time I mindfully choose, I win.

GROWTH
FROM EXPERIENCE

I experience all that is present and soon to be past experiences as a process of growth.
A direct result of this growth is the subtle knowing that this experience too shall come to pass.

LIVE

Live with trust in the abundance you have been bestowed.

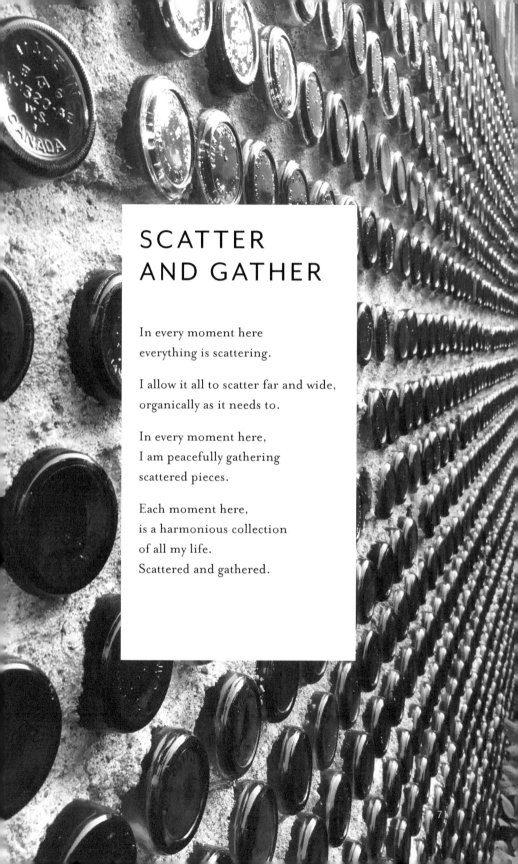

SCATTER AND GATHER

In every moment here
everything is scattering.

I allow it all to scatter far and wide,
organically as it needs to.

In every moment here,
I am peacefully gathering
scattered pieces.

Each moment here,
is a harmonious collection
of all my life.
Scattered and gathered.

HAPPINESS

My version of happiness may not resemble that of another person.

Each human's happiness equation may have varying ratios that depend on the extent of their subscription to ego or spirit.

My place in this life is not to judge this equation. Mine, or theirs.

I am here, only to grow my own happiness story.

Allowing others, the space to grow their own.

LIVING IN SPIRIT

Gratitude for the abundance I have been bestowed.
Forgiveness for the humans who repeatedly choose hate.
Intention to awaken, trust and transform my life.
Joy in the experience of living with love, *kindness and compassion* for myself and all.

THE ESSENCE OF A FEELING

Feelings are perhaps the purest form of Spirit.
Love, fear, anger, sadness, joy, each
in equal intensity are felt in the same way.
They carry the same essence, each a different feeling.

SELF-TALK

Stopping to become aware of that quiet self-talk.
That constant voice in my head.
A voice, so ever present, yet so elusive.
Especially when the narrative is
hateful and loathsome.
Bitter, angry and depreciating.

As I pause, with awareness
I choose to lean into the one listening.
The vulnerable, gullible one.
I notice how she droops with heavy sadness,
as she believes the venomous quiet self-talk.
That's when I know, I must lift her up.
So she may hear,
the magical inner symphony of love,
of compassion, and care.
I must lift her up high, so we may both hear,
the magical love louder than any quiet hateful self-talk.

THE EMBARRASSMENT TRAP

Growing up with constant criticism
perpetuates ego-led fear of embarrassment.

As embarrassment grows into more fear,
the ability to freely create and invent are greatly diminished.

The need to toe the line grows further as ego's bidding is fed.
With it, the capacity to be our true authentic spiritual-self, withers.

Paralyzed with fear, we become incapable of creating anything anymore.
A lull blanket of dullness covers us, and life becomes bland and repetitive.

With immense courage when we challenge our fear of embarrassment,
Arming ourselves with self-acceptance and compassion, we start to
dissolve this fear-based ego trap.

Thus, allowing our authentic creativity to break free and shine through.

THE GAP

The gap between who you are
and who you think you are,
will drive your unconscious choices.
Choices that may not always serve
your best interest.

THE CACTUS FIELDS

In a field where only cactus grow,
    discover the flowers,
        no matter how small or hidden.

Give thanks for their presence,
    appreciate their softness,
        fall in love with their gentleness.

In a field where you were born a cactus,
    grow your soft flowers.

HELP

If you will not
  share with me
   how you want
    to be helped.
No matter what I do,
  you will not
   feel helped
    by me.
The misunderstanding
  between us
   will continue
    to grow.

INNER DIALOGUE

When I was growing up,
several external loud voices told me
that I was useless,
and I wouldn't amount to much.

Within that din, many soft voices whispered to me,
"Keep going, I have you, I support you.
You be all your heart wishes you to be."

Today, I choose to ignore the loud voices who didn't value me.
Instead, I am tuning into the loving whispers, so they may gently
weave into my inner dialogue.

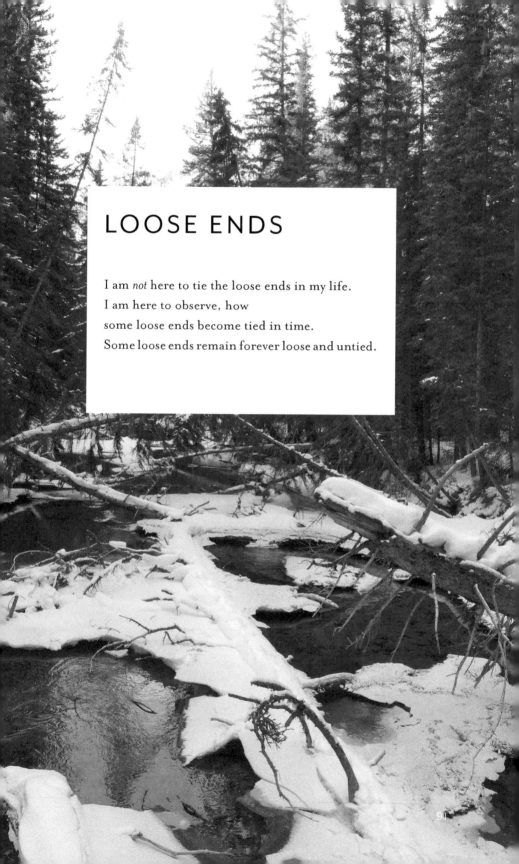

LOOSE ENDS

I am *not* here to tie the loose ends in my life.
I am here to observe, how
some loose ends become tied in time.
Some loose ends remain forever loose and untied.

THE DEATH
OF A FRIENDSHIP

When a friendship starts to die.

I have learnt to give the friend a
universe full of space.

So they may be,
just as they need
to be.

Be all they need to be, in the moment.

As I hold and embrace their *universe*
in my human vessel of *love*.

MINDFUL LIVING REMINDERS

1. No matter what happens to someone or something, I hold within me, the capacity to hold it all with courage and compassion.

2. Life is inherently good and is bringing me all I need.

3. I will trust it all, fall into it, enjoy it fully.

4. I will let go of ego's control of myself, others, and all situations.

5. I will show up, have an enjoyable time with all that is here.

6. Every day I will paint those dreams into reality.

7. Every moment, I will bring my attention to my breathe as I encourage a kind inner narrative.

8. I will allow myself to feel grateful for all that is here and all that is gone now.

9. I will allow my spirit to spread *her* love, far and wide.

10. I will cast out a loving safety net for myself first, before I set one out for anyone else.

96

SUPERPOWER

If I had to choose my superpowers.

I would not choose might or power.
I wound not want to move objects with my mind.

I would choose instead,
to *open with loving kindness,* any closed hearts, and minds.

To *shift with patience* any limited beliefs others hold close.

To *not take* anything too personally.

To be able to *clear* all my ego conditioning.

To *grow and spread into* my vast spiritual space.

To *heal with tenderness* all hurtful wounds.

Mostly, I would choose to *fill cracks in* broken humans with healing golden *love.*

SAPLING

A relationship resembles a vulnerable sapling.
One which relies on resolute gardeners for constant care.
With the aid of unique nutrients such as, love, patience,
acceptance, and forgiveness.
Any relationship will organically thrive and grow.

CHOOSE YOURSELF NOW

In observing those who have aged,
I have learnt many things.

One such important learning is this.

When one has consistently practiced,
choosing their deepest intuitive needs
in their early days.

Those humans could consistently reap the abundant benefits
of this practice in their aging days.

Those humans who did not prioritize
choosing their deepest intuitive needs
in their early days.

They fell prey to a scarcity mindset in their aging days.

Scarcity mindset is the barren ground that *fear* seeks and thrives in.

LETTING BE

I am starting to see the process of *letting go*, as *letting be*.
Patiently, I am residing alongside with all that appears in my life, exactly as it has appeared.
Observing the heavy desire to criticize, judge or change all that has appeared.
With compassion for myself, I am no longer distancing myself, or rejecting the difficult emotions that arise alongside what life has brought to me.
I am openly accepting all of it, with forgiveness, and gratitude.

SURVIVE TO THRIVE

I am examining the coping mechanisms
I adopted to survive difficulties in my younger years.

Now, I choose to thrive than simply survive.

I am replacing the old coping techniques with
patient and peaceful responses.

LIVE
HONESTLY

Respond clearly.
Create freely.
Teach compassionately.
Lead kindly.
Live peacefully.
Engage playfully.
Choose adventurously.
Observe patiently.
Collaborate openly.
Listen attentively.
Seek enthusiastically.
Live honestly.

HEALTHY BOUNDARIES

In this human incarnation,

I have learnt to cast dreams and fantasies aside,
as I choose to set healthy boundaries with others in my life.

I continue to uphold these boundaries,
sometimes with silent amusement.

As I observe the tireless efforts of
the love-bombers and narcissists,
who are determined to make their way back into my life.

MORE ON
HEALTHY BOUNDARIES

Much like forgiveness, setting a healthy boundary can be full of loving kindness. *"I will send you love and light, but I will not allow you back into my life"*.

1. Say *"no"* when you want to say *"no"*.

2. Be *ok* with losing those humans who will not understand or disrespect and question your *"no"*.

3. Know that when they disrespect your *"no"* or question your boundary, you have hit *their* upper limit of growth, not yours.

4. Just because something is *"urgent"* for them, doesn't mean it should become *"urgent"* for you.

5. *Stay true* to yourself, to your heart, to your inner voice, no matter how lonely your life feels for a while.

6. Know that if you *set the intention* to be surrounded by humans who truly *love you*, *care for* your wellbeing, *respect* your life and needs, *support* your dreams and creations, *choose* to be around you, and are *available* to you. The *universe* will bring them to you. With patience, keep setting those healthy boundaries.

NOW

It's all happening here, *now*.
The past is now, the future is now.
In their own planes of existence,
they occur simultaneously.

In parallel.
Now.

It is *now* that I make memories.
When I am awake and aware,
I choose to make joyous memories.
When I am asleep in ego dreams,
my memories are saddened
by shadow self.

My memories like my dreams
are a glimpse across the veil.
The veil that keeps hidden the many planes
of past, present, and future.

Now, is all that exists.

DIFFICULT WOMAN

I strengthen the health of my personal boundaries,
by growing closer to my authentic self and revising their limits.

Those humans, who had been previously allowed
across my boundary, to throw unkind tantrums at me,
are now kindly uninvited.

They are the first to deem me a difficult woman.

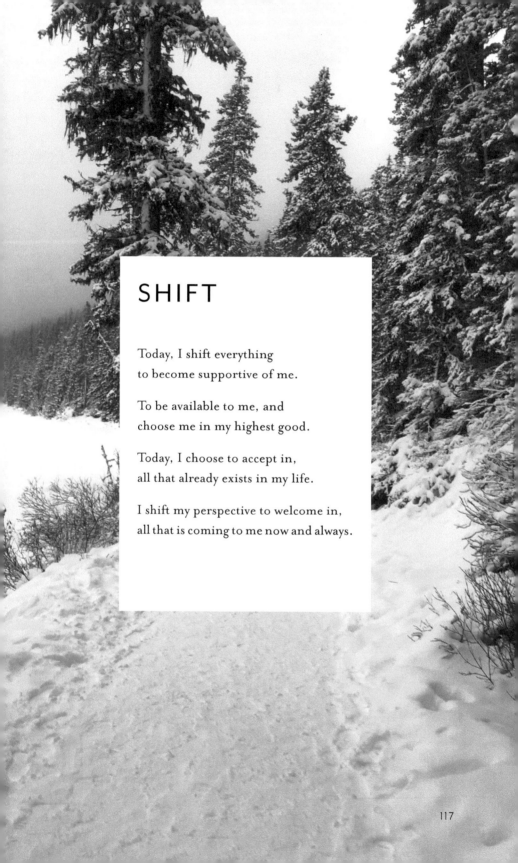

SHIFT

Today, I shift everything
to become supportive of me.

To be available to me, and
choose me in my highest good.

Today, I choose to accept in,
all that already exists in my life.

I shift my perspective to welcome in,
all that is coming to me now and always.

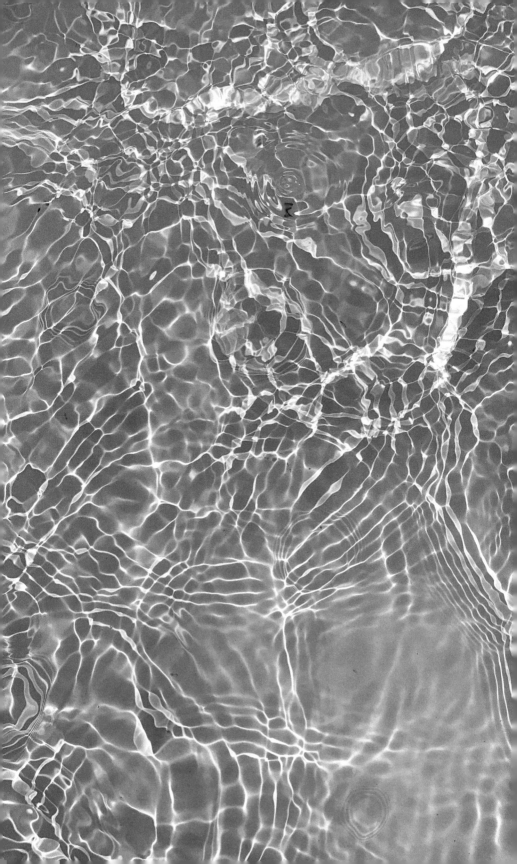

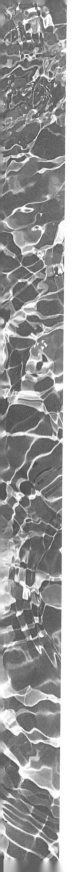

Smriti Agrawal, PhD, is a transformation teacher. She helps people find their authentic selves so that they may grow and live happier lives. Her poetry first appeared in daily meditations she shared with clients. Inspired by their appreciation of these affirmations, Smriti collected her poems into *Awaken Trust Transform Live* so that more people may find self-healing.

She lives in Calgary, Alberta, with her daughter and her dog Max. This is her first book. For more information on Smriti's workshops, Reiki healing, and resources, you can visit her website: www.smritiagrawal.com.

V/55